ECOSYSTEMS OF THE WORLD

OCEAN ECOSYSTEMS

by Pam Watts

Content Consultant
Erin L. Meyer-Gutrob
PhD Candidate, Oceanography
Cornell University

Core Library

An Imprint of Abdo Publishing
abdopublishing.com

abdopublishing.com

Published by Abdo Publishing, a division of ABDO, PO Box 398166, Minneapolis, Minnesota 55439. Copyright © 2016 by Abdo Consulting Group, Inc. International copyrights reserved in all countries. No part of this book may be reproduced in any form without written permission from the publisher. Core Library™ is a trademark and logo of Abdo Publishing.

Printed in the United States of America, North Mankato, Minnesota
042015
092015

THIS BOOK CONTAINS
RECYCLED MATERIALS

Cover Photo: iStockphoto
Interior Photos: iStockphoto, 1, 10, 15, 18, 31 (top), 31 (lower middle), 36, 38, 45; Shutterstock Images, 4, 31 (upper middle), 31 (right), 43; Jolanta Wojcicka/Shutterstock Images, 7; Rich Carey/Shutterstock Images, 12, 31 (left); Ralph White/Corbis, 16; Bryan Toro/iStockphoto, 20; NASA/Zuma Press/Newscom, 23; Flip Nicklin/Minden Pictures/ Corbis, 26; Angelo Giampiccolo/Shutterstock Images, 28; Corey Ford/iStockphoto, 31 (bottom); Flip Nicklin/Minden Pictures/Newscom, 32; Peter Bennett/Ambient Images/ Newscom, 35

Editor: Jon Westmark
Series Designer: Becky Daum

Library of Congress Control Number: 2015931583

Cataloging-in-Publication Data
Watts, Pam.
 Ocean ecosystems / Pam Watts.
   p. cm. -- (Ecosystems of the world)
Includes bibliographical references and index.
ISBN 978-1-62403-855-6
1. Marine ecology--Juvenile literature.   2. Oceans--Juvenile literature.   I. Title.
577.7--dc23
                                                    2015931583

CONTENTS

CHAPTER ONE

LIFE IN THE OCEAN

The sea is warm and still. A golden-brown carpet of seaweed called sargassum stretches along the surface. The bed of seaweed is part of the Sargasso Sea in the North Atlantic Ocean. It is the best hiding spot for animals living in the open ocean.

A young loggerhead turtle rests inside the sargassum. It eats smaller creatures, such as shrimp, fish, crabs, and snails that hide among the weeds.

Sargassum floats near the surface in large island-like pieces.

These creatures, in turn, eat smaller organisms, most often the microscopic phytoplankton. Phytoplankton make food from sunlight with the help of nutrients from the bodies and feces of larger organisms.

High above the surface of the sea, a predatory bird soars. A shark circles 300 feet (91 m) below the surface. These animals are a threat to the loggerhead. They often eat turtles. But the loggerhead is safe in the open ocean.

Ocean Diversity

The Sargasso Sea is one ocean habitat. But there are many others. The ocean covers nearly 75

A Long Journey

Some ocean species remain in the same habitat their entire lives. Others travel thousands of miles each year. This is called transoceanic migration. The main reasons for migration are to find food and to reproduce. Many baby sea turtles emerge from nests on the Gulf Coast in Florida each year. They swim to the powerful Gulf Stream. This current takes them to the Sargasso Sea. Here they live out their young lives hidden amongst the seaweed. When they reach adulthood, some of the females travel back to the same beach where they hatched to lay their own eggs.

Coral reefs cover less than one percent of the seafloor. But they support approximately 25 percent of ocean creatures.

percent of Earth. It is very diverse. It stretches from the icy polar regions to the sun-warmed equator. It creeps along coastlines in what are called intertidal zones. It supports coral reefs, often called rain forests of the sea because of their diversity. The open ocean, called the pelagic zone, is home to many species. And in the deep sea, unique organisms live and breathe. Most of the ocean is unexplored. But we know it is home to millions of strange and wonderful species. Some ocean organisms have adapted to survive in

The Ocean and Earth

All life on Earth depends on the ocean. Microscopic plants in the ocean, called phytoplankton, create more than half of the planet's oxygen. The ocean helps regulate the weather, water, and nutrients Earth's organisms need to survive. The ocean also keeps Earth at a moderate temperature that allows life to exist.

regions without oxygen. Others can see in places with almost no light. Some creatures can withstand thousands of pounds of water pushing down on them. Each species has evolved to survive in its unique environment, and each one plays an important role in the ecosystem.

Learning and Protecting

Some human actions, such as deep sea oil drilling and polluting, are hurting the ocean. The ocean is largely unexplored. So scientists are unsure of how much damage humans have caused. Many people are working to protect the sea. But this can be difficult because most of the ocean is not owned by any one country.

In 2000 a panel of ocean experts prepared a report for the US president on the importance of ocean exploration:

> We cannot protect what we do not know, and thus, without ocean exploration, we are ignorant of what needs to be conserved in a realm that covers most of the surface of the Earth. The ocean provides a bounty of renewable resources, but without knowledge of what's out there, how abundant it is, and how quickly it is replenished, we cannot plan for its environmentally sustainable use. Every day, governments make decisions on how to best regulate the use of the oceans, yet they lack the basic knowledge to make informed choices.
>
> Source: President's Panel for Oceanic Exploration. Discovering Earth's Final Frontier: A U.S. Strategy for Ocean Exploration. Washington, DC: US Department of Commerce, 2000. PDF file.

What's the Big Idea?

Take a close look at the excerpt. What are the ocean experts trying to tell the president? What arguments do they use to make their point? How do you think their focus would change if they were presenting a report to another group of scientists?

CHAPTER TWO

EXTREME CONDITIONS

Ocean organisms have evolved to live in specific conditions. These conditions vary widely in different parts of the ocean.

The most important factor for any organism is food. Sunlight is the main energy source in the ocean. It drives photosynthesis. Photosynthesis is the process by which certain organisms, such as plants, use nutrients and sunlight to create food. Without

With good weather conditions, giant kelp can grow up to two feet (0.6 m) per day.

Bluefish tuna use the currents in the Atlantic Ocean to migrate for food and to spawn.

this process, life as we know it would not exist on Earth. But sunlight does not penetrate deeply into the ocean. So organisms that make food from the sun live at the surface. These organisms grow mostly in spring and summer, when there are many hours of sunlight.

Pelagic Waters

In the open ocean, temperatures are often warm near the surface, where sunlight is abundant. This allows photosynthesizing organisms to grow quickly most of the year. Creatures that feed on them thrive as well.

The Sargasso Sea is an example of an open ocean ecosystem. It is the only sea that does not touch land. Instead it is surrounded by a system of currents called the North Atlantic Gyre. Currents are similar to rivers. They move faster than the surrounding water. Gyres are sets of rotating ocean currents. They transport water in a vortex around a still, inner region called a convergence zone. There are five major ocean gyres. They carry heat and nutrients from one place to another. They also trap things inside. Certain creatures

The Gulf Stream Current

The Gulf Stream is a powerful current. It flows along the east coast of North America. It forms the western edge of the North Atlantic Gyre. The Gulf Stream moves more water per second than the biggest 20 rivers in the world combined. It carries animals and seaweed. It also moves human waste products that do not disintegrate easily. These items collect in the same still waters that are vital for many ocean animals. One of the ocean's "garbage patches" is in the North Atlantic Gyre.

have adapted to live in the still waters of the Sargasso Sea, especially young, vulnerable animals, such as baby eels and sea turtles.

Polar Waters

Polar waters, such as the Arctic and Southern Oceans, are known for their icy temperatures. Animals living here must adapt to the cold. Walruses and other polar mammals have large stores of fat that help them stay warm. Other animals have substances in their blood that keep them from freezing.

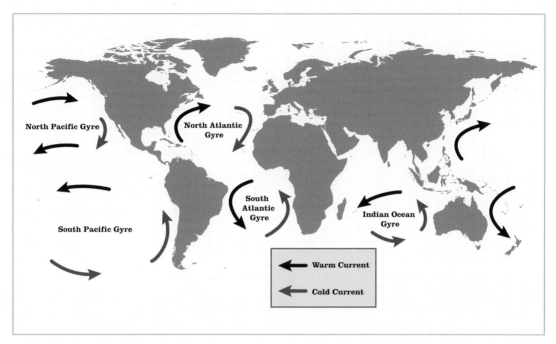

Ocean Currents

This map shows the major ocean gyres. These are places where still water is surrounded by currents. How does the map compare to what you have read in the text? Does it help you understand how both organisms and trash collect in certain parts of the ocean?

Arctic animals often lack food sources. Winter days in arctic regions do not have enough hours of sunlight to support photosynthesis. For this reason, many animals, such as certain whale species, only live in polar areas in the summer. They migrate in the winter.

Vents called black smokers occur when hot fluids from under Earth's crust mix with near-freezing seawater.

Deep Sea

There are some regions where photosynthesis is impossible. One place is the deep sea, where no sunlight is available. The organisms here find other ways to get energy. Some eat waste products from other ocean organisms. Others eat oil found near the ocean floor. Some eat chemicals that rise up from cracks in the seafloor. These cracks are called hydrothermal vents. The water at the vents mixes with magma under Earth's crust, causing temperatures to reach up to 750 degrees Fahrenheit (400°C).

Water pressure also controls which creatures can live in the deep sea. The deeper the water, the more pressure it exerts. Organisms that live or hunt in the deep sea have different bodies than those that live in shallow water. For example, sperm whales have collapsible ribcages and lungs. This allows them to hunt giant squids at depths of 7,000 feet (2,134 m). A human's bones would snap from the pressure at that depth.

Some species of sea stars live in intertidal waters. Sea stars have suckers on the ends of their arms they use to attach to rocks.

Intertidal Zones

Intertidal zones are regions along coastlines where the ocean flows alongside the land. Intertidal zones are rich with nutrients from the land. Photosynthesis is often strong here.

All the organisms living in intertidal zones must be able to survive both in and out of the water. This is because they have to deal with powerful tides that cause them to spend part of their time on land and the other part in the sea. Eelgrass, mussels, anemones, and sea stars anchor onto rocks or the sea floor as the tides rush in and out.

Coral Reefs

The most diverse ocean ecosystems are coral reefs. Coral reefs form in shallow, warm waters that support photosynthesis year round. Coral is a type of animal. The coral that makes up the structure of a reef is hard and stony. It builds on older and dead coral. Other animals gather at the reef. Many use it for shelter.

CHAPTER THREE

PRODUCERS

All living things on Earth are part of food chains. At the bottom of every food chain are organisms known as producers. Plants make up the largest group of producers on land. They take light from the sun and nutrients from the soil, which they use to make food. Then animals eat them. The ocean does not have many plants compared with other ecosystems. There are few places in the ocean where plants can take root

Eelgrass is one ocean plant. Its roots help hold the ground in place and prevent erosion in tidal areas.

and stretch toward the sun. This means animals must get their food from other sources.

Microscopic phytoplankton solve this problem. They are the main producers in the ocean. Phytoplankton take energy from the sun and nutrients from the water to make food and oxygen. They live along the surface of the water and bloom where nutrients and sunshine are abundant. Scientists estimate phytoplankton generate 50 to 85 percent of Earth's oxygen.

Seaweed is another producer in the ocean.

Phytoplankton

Massive blooms of phytoplankton are a natural feature of the open ocean and coastal waters. The blooms can be as large as 96,526 square miles (250,000 sq km). Their color depends on the species. Some paint the surface of the water in greens, blues, whites, yellows, and turquoises. These blooms are mostly healthy for the ecosystem. Some blooms are a rusty red color similar to blood. These toxic blooms are known as red tide. They create compounds that are extremely harmful to marine animals and humans.

Phytoplankton blooms can sometimes be seen from outer space.

23

Scientists do not classify seaweed as a plant because it is made of algae. This means every part of seaweed can photosynthesize instead of just the leaves. Seaweed does not have roots. But most seaweed still connects to the ground and stretches toward sunlight. Some pieces stretch approximately 300 feet (91 m).

Seaweed

Seaweed looks similar to plants. But it operates differently. Most seaweed anchors to the ground. The anchor is called a holdfast. The stem and leaves of seaweed are called the stipe and the blades. Seaweed falls over without water. It has a small pocket of air called an air bladder at the base of each blade. The air bladder makes the blades lighter than the surrounding water so they can stretch toward the sun.

Eelgrass and mangroves are two plants that grow in the ocean. Eelgrass grows near the coast. It has strong roots that hold it in place through the changing tides. Mangroves live along tropical coastlines. Their roots arch up above the ground. This allows water to flow freely without uprooting the trees.

Some researchers believe that other planets may have developed life in their deep seas similar to the life that exists around Earth's deep-sea hydrothermal vents. NASA researcher Max Coleman says in an interview:

> It's difficult to think that our ocean on earth could be a good analogue for something like an icy moon of Jupiter—which is as small as our moon, has an ocean which goes up to eight or nine times as deep as ours, and has an icy shell on the surface. . . . Well it could be, because although the gravity is less there, it's deeper, and therefore the pressure at the bottom of Europa's ocean is effectively the same as we get at the bottom of our oceans here, where there is life. And it's also got oxygen in it as our oceans do near the bottom.
>
> Source: Max Coleman. "Looking for Life in Oceans on Earth and in Space." Aquarium of the Pacific. Aquarium of the Pacific, November 19, 2014. Web. Accessed February 25, 2015.

What's the Big Idea?
Take a closer look at the passage above. What is Coleman's main idea? What evidence does he use to support this point?

CHAPTER FOUR

CONSUMERS, SCAVENGERS, AND DECOMPOSERS

Producers bring energy into ecosystems. Consumers help transfer the energy through the ecosystem. They eat producers and other consumers to survive. Animals that eat producers are called primary consumers.

Phytoplankton are so small they can only be seen through a powerful microscope. Most primary consumers also are very small. They are called

Krill are particularly important in the Antarctic food chain, where they feed on ice algae and other plankton.

27

zooplankton. Krill are an example of zooplankton.
They are shrimp-like creatures approximately the
size of a paper clip. Jellyfish are another type of
zooplankton. They are much larger than krill. But like
all zooplankton, jellyfish are drifters. They float much
more than they swim.

Animals that eat zooplankton are secondary
consumers. Blue whales are secondary consumers.

They eat approximately four tons (3.6 metric tons) of krill per day. Blue whales do not have any major natural predators. But other secondary consumers, such as small fish and sea turtles, are often eaten by larger predators.

Some predators have a very big impact on the other species in the ecosystem. These are known as keystone species. Sometimes keystone species are at the top of the food chain, such as sharks. But other animals, such as

A Delicate Balance

Populations of different species are finely tuned to each other in the ocean. If a keystone species disappears, the entire ecosystem undergoes a drastic change. For example, the sea otter eats about a quarter of its body weight daily. It eats nearly anything it can find, but it prefers urchins. In the 1800s, otters were hunted nearly to extinction along the Pacific Coast. The urchin population significantly increased and ate all the seaweed in the region. When otters were reintroduced, the urchin population decreased. The seaweed came back, along with the fish, seabirds, and seals that depended on it.

Camouflage

Many marine animals use camouflage to hide. In the Sargasso Sea, animals often blend in with the seaweed. The sargassum fish, for instance, has fleshy, seaweed-like knobs. These help make it one of the most successful predators in the Sargasso Sea, even though the fish is only six inches (15 cm) long. Another master of disguise is the octopus. This colorblind animal can change the color and texture of its skin to match its surroundings. Scientists are still trying to figure out how it does this.

the sea otter, can also be keystone species.

Cleaning Up

Some organisms eat whatever they can find. They are called scavengers, and they play an important role in the ocean. Scavengers help make sure nothing goes to waste. They feed on dead organisms or waste products from other organisms that fall to the ocean floor. Crabs and sharks are scavengers.

Sharks are also top predators. They eat other predators and herbivores.

Organisms such as fungi and sea slugs are called decomposers. They feed on ocean waste. When

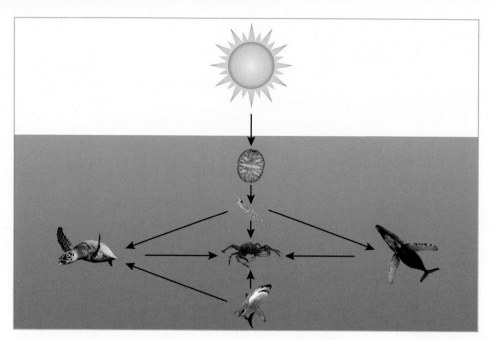

An Ocean Food Web
The ocean food web includes species both large and small. Animals from sea turtles to blue whales eat zooplankton, such as krill. Krill eat tiny phytoplankton, which make their own food using the sun. Sharks are top predators. And crabs scavenge the remains of dead organisms. How does this food web help you understand the flow of energy in the ocean?

whales and other large animals die, their carcasses can support many scavengers and decomposers. Other organisms eat the scavengers and decomposers. This keeps the energy from the dead animal in the ecosystem. The complex set of interactions that cycle energy throughout the ecosystem is called the food web.

CHAPTER FIVE

PEOPLE AND THE OCEAN

The ocean contains many finely tuned ecosystems. However, these ecosystems are vulnerable to change. Humans are affecting the ocean in many ways. For instance, humans hunt ocean animals for food, pelts, and blubber. People sometimes overhunt ocean animals. The animals cannot reproduce quickly enough. Their numbers go down. Many species, including blue whales, are almost extinct as a result.

Blue whales are the largest animals on Earth. They can grow up to 100 feet (30 m) long.

Shipping Containers

Sometimes very large forms of human waste end up in the ocean. About 10,000 20-foot-long (6.1-m) shipping containers fall off ships each year. These containers are used for transporting goods across the ocean. Some contain toxic chemicals. Others carry less harmful objects. Scientists are studying how the containers affect ocean ecosystems. A container carrying tires was discovered in the ocean in 2004. It was found off the coast of California. The container provides a habitat for many species. Sea snails and octopuses live around it. Sunken ships often serve a similar role.

One of the biggest ways humans affect the ocean is by polluting it. Garbage collects inside gyres. Each ocean gyre has a garbage patch. But the biggest is the Great Pacific Garbage Patch in the center of the North Pacific Gyre. It is thought to be larger than the United States.

Fertilizer is another form of human waste found in the ocean. It has a big impact on ocean ecosystems. Producers in the ocean need nutrients to grow. Fertilizers provide nutrients that help

Scientists collect water samples from the North Pacific Gyre. Much of the garbage in the gyre is tiny plastic.

some types of phytoplankton bloom. This can have a number of harmful effects. Areas that bloom too much take oxygen out of the water. This creates dead zones where nothing else can grow. It also leads to toxic blooms, such as red tide.

Oil Spills

Another man-made pollutant found in the ocean is oil. *Deepwater Horizon*, an oil rig located in the Gulf of Mexico, blew up in 2010. It caused the biggest oil

Oil can make it difficult for turtles to breathe. It can also damage their internal organs when swallowed.

spill in history. It took almost three months to stop the oil from flowing into the ocean. By then more than 200 million gallons (757 million L) of oil had leaked into the Gulf. Oil is known to kill many creatures. The long-term effects of oil spills, especially the *Deepwater Horizon* spill, are largely unknown. One study showed 17 percent of dolphins in an affected area off the coast of Louisiana were sick in 2011. Many endangered sea turtles were stranded on shore because of the oil.

Oceans have an amazing capacity to heal themselves. After the *Deepwater Horizon* spill, the biggest cleanup effort was carried out by bacteria. Some oil occurs naturally in the Gulf. A few species of bacteria have evolved to eat it. After the spill, scientists sprayed the ocean with compounds that broke up the oil. The bacteria then took over. They multiplied quickly and ate the oil. They cleaned much of the area. But the bacteria used up a great deal of the oxygen in the water. This enlarged the Gulf's dead zone.

FURTHER EVIDENCE

Chapter Five talks about several ways humans affect ocean ecosystems. What is the main point of the chapter? What evidence in the text supports this point? Visit the website below to learn more about garbage patches. Choose a quotation from the website that relates to this chapter. Does this quotation support the author's main point? Does it make a new point? Write a few sentences explaining how the quotation you found relates to this chapter.

Trash Plaguing Our Sea
mycorelibrary.com/ocean-ecosystems

CHAPTER SIX

THE FUTURE
OF THE OCEAN

The future of the ocean is uncertain. Humans are polluting ocean ecosystems. But climate change also may have a big impact on the future of the ocean. Ocean organisms are used to specific temperatures. If the ocean warms even a few degrees, it may have a huge effect on much of the life in the seas. Gray whales, for instance, have begun to delay their migration south as a result of warming waters.

Lobsters are cold-blooded. Their body temperature changes with the water around them. Slight changes in temperature could force lobsters to migrate to cooler waters.

Water expands as it warms. And as Earth warms, the polar ice caps are starting to melt. These two factors cause sea levels to rise. Higher water levels could have a big impact on organisms that are sensitive to water depth, such as coral.

Excess carbon dioxide in the atmosphere dissolves in the ocean. This makes the water more acidic and affects some ocean animals. For example, it hurts mollusks' ability to build shells. This leaves them exposed to other animals.

One problem people have in trying to protect the ocean is that no one owns it. Approximately

Population Mystery

Sometimes humans cause ocean populations to decline without knowing it. The yellow-eye rockfish was severely overfished in 2001. Its population was estimated to be only 7 to 13 percent of its original numbers. This surprised people because the yellow-eye is not often fished. Scientists discovered fishing hurts the species because many of the fish are caught before they are old enough to reproduce. These fish can live for more than 100 years, and they reproduce late in life.

50 percent of the ocean is outside any nation's legal control. A few multinational organizations, such as Oceana and the Sargasso Sea Alliance, are working to protect uncontrolled areas.

Most ecosystems have some ability to adapt to change. The ocean is no exception. But like all ecosystems, there is a delicate balance that needs to be maintained. The future of the ocean may look very different if changes continue to disturb the balance.

EXPLORE ONLINE

The focus of Chapter Six is the future of the ocean. This chapter discusses how climate change may impact the ocean. The website below also focuses on climate change and the ocean. As you know, every source is different. How is the information given in the website different from the information in this chapter? Which information is the same? How do the two sources present information differently? What can you learn from this website?

New England Aquarium: Climate Change
mycorelibrary.com/ocean-ecosystems

Atlantic Ocean

This ocean is located off the eastern coast of North America and reaches all the way to Europe and Africa. It is home to the Gulf of Mexico and the Sargasso Sea. The longest mountain chain on Earth stretches underwater across the center of the Atlantic.

Indian Ocean

The Indian Ocean lies between Africa and Australia. It is the third-largest ocean. The Indian Ocean is the warmest ocean. The warm water keeps phytoplankton growth lower than other oceans. With fewer producers, life does not thrive in many parts of the Indian Ocean.

Pacific Ocean

This ocean stretches from the western coast of North America to Asia and Australia. It is the biggest ocean. It includes the deepest point on Earth, the Mariana Trench. Hawaii and some of the most active volcanoes on Earth are found in the Pacific.

Polar bears hunt seals by waiting for them to surface. Seals are polar bears' main food source.

The Polar Oceans

These are the Arctic and Southern Oceans. They are near the North and South Poles and are the coldest oceans. They are home to many species that are adapted to cold conditions, such as penguins, polar bears, whales, walruses, and seals.

You Are There

Imagine you are a sea turtle that has just hatched on the Gulf Coast of Florida. You race across the beach and into the water. Soon you are in the Gulf Stream. What does it feel like to be carried along in the current? What other organisms do you see as you hide in the seaweed?

Say What?

Studying ecosystems means learning a great deal of new vocabulary. Find five words in this book you have never seen before. Then use a dictionary to find out what they mean. Write the definitions in your own words, and use them in sentences.

GLOSSARY

consumer
an organism that cannot create the nutrients it needs

decomposer
an organism that breaks down organic material, such as dead organisms

extinction
the complete disappearance of a species from Earth

food chain
a series of organisms each dependent on the next as a source of food

habitat
a place or a type of place where an organism lives

intertidal zone
the area of shoreline between low and high tides

keystone species
a species that affects many other species in the ecosystem

photosynthesis
a process in which producers use sunlight to create food

phytoplankton
small, drifting producers found in the ocean

predator
an animal that kills and eats other animals

producer
an organism that uses solar energy or chemical energy to create the food it needs

zooplankton
small, floating herbivores that feed on phytoplankton

LEARN MORE

Books

Hague, Bradley. *Alien Deep: Revealing the Mysterious Living World at the Bottom of the Ocean.* Washington, DC: National Geographic, 2012.

Rizzo, Johnna. *Oceans: Dolphins, Sharks Penguins, and More!* Washington, DC: National Geographic, 2010.

Websites

To learn more about Ecosystems of the World, visit **booklinks.abdopublishing.com**. These links are routinely monitored and updated to provide the most current information available.

Visit **mycorelibrary.com** for free additional tools for teachers and students.

INDEX

ABOUT THE AUTHOR

Pam Watts grew up on the Gulf Coast of Florida. She spent her childhood swimming and boating in the ocean. She now lives in New Mexico, where she watches coyotes and mountain lions instead of manatees and sea turtles.

Surprise Me

Chapter Five describes ways humans are changing the ocean. After reading this book, what two or three facts about the ways we are affecting the ocean surprised you most? Write a few sentences about each fact. Why did they surprise you?

Take a Stand

Many parts of the ocean are not under the care of a particular nation. Who should be responsible for protecting these areas? Write a short essay explaining your opinion. Make sure to support your opinion with details and facts.